Advance Praise

In *Meadows of Memory* Danuta E. Kosk-Kosicka shows a poet's love and commitment, translating her own Mother's stories and poetry from Polish to English. She opens a portal for Lidia Kosk to cast a spell of folklore, fairytale and imagined worlds. Creativity is beauty in truth, and Danuta E. Kosk-Kosicka makes another writer's inner values and humanity wonderfully available. This collaboration, with Mother Lidia Kosk seen through a daughter's prism, is realization and richness at once.

— Grace Cavalieri, *The Poet and the Poem from the Library of Congress*

Filled with lyricism and hard-won wisdom, this volume of poems and fable-like reminiscences of childhood and war boomerangs our way across decades and continents. What lands before us, "tossed like a prize," is a marvel of beauty that testifies to the incorruptibility of the human spirit. Lidia Kosk's pastoral portraits of "wind / horses / people," deftly translated from Polish by her daughter, exist in the liminal space between dream and reality, where we go to steady our thoughts. Like the human breath or the "strokes of the church clock / from a faraway tower," Kosk's words "organize time" and in doing so shed light on the human condition, including the moment when "birds fall silent / the human voice softens." If we, the readers who "look at the world from an upright position," ever find ourselves at the spot "where the train tracks end," let's hope it's with *Meadows of Memory* in our knapsacks.

— Piotr Florczyk, author of *East & West*, translator of *Building the Barricade* by Anna Świrszczyńska

These pieces, salvaged from the complexities of a life's long journey, cross borders of time and space, landscapes and loves. Their narratives invite us to witness to the wonderful imagination of a child who later becomes an adult experiencing feelings that "stream in from faraway times/ Shadows… in the meadows of remembrance." The works invite the question what is memory? as they "look at clouds like angel's wings / Still laden with yesterday's toils and tears." From a childhood on distant soil, through confusion and grief, survival and love, these pieces track the travels of an indomitable spirit and demonstrate ways that memory serves us as a "shield against forgetting."

—Michael S. Glaser, Poet Laureate of Maryland 2004-2009

Poet Danuta E. Kosk-Kosicka's deeply moving latest book, *Meadows of Memory*, delights the mind, heart, and senses with its masterly Polish-to-English translation of her mother's poems and stories dating from the start of what will be World War Two.

Translation: 1. the act of putting words into a different language. 2. the act of moving a work from one form into another.

In *Meadows of Memory: Poems and Prose* by Lidia Kosk, Danuta E. Kosk-Kosicka has done both. As her daughter, Danuta knows Lidia's voice intimately—how it sounds in their native Polish, how it sounds spoken aloud. How it means. Thus the poems and stories embody an intimacy and immediacy which take them to the second definition: the translation of Lidia Kosk's voice into something the reader hears, feels, smells, touches. In the meadows is "a terrified bird" trembling "in the trapping hands," a "hare's terrified heartbeat." Over summer meadows was "a burning in the sky" proclaiming "there will be war." The two writers, mother and daughter, translate us directly—almost bodily—into those meadows' terror and beauty.

—Clarinda Harriss, publisher of BrickHouse Books, Inc., author of *Innumerable Moons*

The unique poems and prose of Lidia Kosk are marked by a generational form of East European surrealism first introduced to Americans by Robert Hass and Charles Simic. Redolent with mysterious memories of her Polish childhood and a life lived in peace and turmoil (see "I Patted a Hedgehog"), her work freely mixes reality and imagination. She herself titles one poem "Dream or Not a Dream." Her dreamscapes feel like fairy tales in which vegetation and animals, hares, pheasants, dogs, turtles, and frogs, horses especially, play prominent roles. Dissociation from the everyday is further heightened by the way she speaks of herself in the third person as "Lidia" or "the girl." The punchy brevity, expert use of slant rhyme and line breaks, an almost uniform absence of punctuation, her aphoristic titles and brave endings, all serve to accentuate the power of her poems. And Lidia Kosk has the very good luck of being translated by her daughter, two poets genetically and stylistically linked.

—Michael Salcman, editor of the anthology *Poetry in Medicine*,
author of *A Prague Spring, Before & After*

Meadows of Memory

Meadows of Memory

Poems and Prose by
Lidia Kosk

Selected and Translated by
Danuta E. Kosk-Kosicka

Apprentice
House Press
Loyola University Maryland

First Edition

Paperback ISBN: 978-1-62720-233-6
Ebook ISBN: 978-1-62720-234-3

Printed in the United States of America

Development & design by Olivia Airhart
Promotions editor: Claire Riley

Published by Apprentice House Press

Apprentice
House Press
Loyola University Maryland

Apprentice House Press
Loyola University Maryland
4501 N. Charles Street
Baltimore, MD 21210
410.617.5265 • 410.617.2198 (fax)
www.ApprenticeHouse.com
info@ApprenticeHouse.com

To Grażyna—daughter to the author, sister to the translator

Contents

I

Lily

Tosia, pregnant with her third child, walked back home on the path that led through the marshland. Her husband, Antosiek, drove the cart on a nearby road. Afraid of the jolts of the cart, Tosia preferred to walk the shortcut. The marshes attracted her. She enjoyed the scents, charm, quiet, and beauty of the flowers.

A particular white lily on the very edge of a pond caught her attention. It seemed to grow right at arm's length. Leaning over the water, Tosia grabbed the stem and lost her balance. She managed to scream. Fortunately, at that moment Antosiek was within earshot and ran to pull her out.

Back in the cart in her sopping dress, she clutched the lily in one hand while holding onto the seat with the other. With every jump of the cart, Tosia was filled with concern for her baby. When they arrived home, Antosiek had to lift her from the cart and carry her in his arms into the house. Grandmother Agnieszka immediately started preparations to deliver the baby. "Get the water boiling, fast!" she shouted to Antosiek.

With some difficulty, Agnieszka extracted the white lily from the clenched fist of the young woman in childbirth. Tosia managed to whisper weakly, "Put the flower in cold water."

The baby girl was named Lily. The parish priest did not approve of the name, but Tosia refused to give in. She kept the white lily for a long time in a vase filled with water from the marshes.

Little Lily—called Lilijka by her grandmother—was growing up and maturing quickly; she was lean, lithe, and resilient. Her curious, russet-and-green-hued eyes seemed to change, depending on the colors of her surroundings. Green complimented her face. Intense red caused her eyes to appear as if they were gazing up from under deep water. Her face shone with beauty, attracting the attention of those around her.

Tosia was very busy raising her children, taking care of the house and the farm, and sometimes also helping her husband in his hard work. Less and less often was she able to visit the marshland; in the end she would come only when no one could help Antosiek cut the peat in the water. After she gave birth to two more children, she couldn't go anymore.

On the day Lilijka turned five, she heard from Grandma Agnieszka about the events preceding her birth. That night, Lilijka dreamed about a white lily in a vase. In the morning, she woke up with the strong conviction that she had seen that lily. She was even able to smell the mysterious marshes. "I need to go to the marshland," she said to her grandmother, with whom she shared a special bond. Grandma consented.

When they reached the pond from which Tosia had taken the beautiful flower, her little daughter heard the water murmur: *Look at your reflection in me, lean closer, move closer to me.* Lilijka felt herself being pulled in. She felt joyful, light as a feather; she wanted to fly. She saw her reflection at the same time as her grandmother did. Grandma caught her by the hand and pulled her close, calling the girl to return. For a few more moments, Lilijka felt herself floating over the undulating green carpet of marsh grass decorated with amaranthine flowers and droplets of water glistening like tiny mirrors.

Never again was Lily able to enter that enchanted world, but it remained with her. It came to life in her grandmother's tales of the land, tales in which fen-fire featured prominently. The mysterious master of the realm of marshes, bogs, and fens seized Lily's imagination. He appeared to her by turns as a whirling glimmer or an errant spirit. "Grandma, why are people in your stories afraid of him?" she would ask.

And thus she heard that the spirit of the fenland punishes those who venture into his territory. He lures them, mesmerizes them, now blazing like a torch and tempting them to follow, now splitting into minute, quivering flickers. Anyone who has seen such lights wandering the swamp or purple-blue flames suddenly creeping out from under the clumps of vegetation talks about them with delight. Only the traveller's memory of the instant when the green grass upon which he steps transforms into a vortex of sticky mud sucking him in with paralyzing force reminds him of the horror. How fortunate are those who manage to find strength in their arms to pull themselves up from the trap. "Walking in the marshland is treacherous," added Grandma, looking into Lilijka's glowing eyes.

Years later, Lily realized that the images and the marsh-scented breeze kept coming back to her. They gave her extra strength in difficult times. Sometimes they foretold future events.

Once, surrounded by the walls of a crowded city, she woke up at dawn. From the open window, a light mist of morning dew floated towards her and through her, filling the room with a familiar scent. As the dew slowly dissipated, these lines came to her:

Led by a pathway until now unknown,
I enter the marshland, scent of herbs and peat.
Stay straight on the path, leave the flowers alone
Where churning forces await misguided feet!

To possess secret realms, treacherous, mighty,
My legs take me to where the end unveils.
Drawn in by delusions, beguiling, delighting,
Imagination feeds on overheard tales.

Drifting vapors bedew luxuriant grass blades
Silver-plated by drops, abundant and sweet.
A white figure emerges, draped in haze and shade
Summoning or demanding my retreat?

The swaying, bowing haze swirls through the realm
Spreads a gauzy shawl on the slippery tract.
The words unfurl: here Master Fen-Fire reigns.
Consider retreating a courageous act.

White Horses in the White Grove

The galloping of a carefree foal
in an enchanted circle of closeness to its mother
remains an indestructible image
in Lidia's soul.

Along the road lined with willow trees to the dirt road skirting the marshes, Lidia would fall asleep on the wobbling, four-board cart to the sound of rattling wheels. She would awaken when the cart reached the meadow with a large pear tree in the middle. Lidia went there several times with her father to gather the round pears that—spread out in the attic—in just a short time turned into tasty *ulęgałki*. At the meadow there would always be a warm welcome from two elderly people. Lidia wished she could visit them more often. Some kind of secret surrounded them. Later, she could not recall how she had been instructed to address them. Maybe they were her father's parents? But she had heard that those grandparents had died much earlier during a typhoid epidemic, when her little brother Rysio had also died after suckling the disease with the milk from his mother's typhus-riddled breast. Daddy's sister had brought the illness to the family. Nevertheless, his family blamed Lidia's mother for Rysio's death. She never regained her lust for life. Daddy's family did not like her, probably because they thought that she was rich. Lidia's mom never bragged about her wealth; she was very modest. She suffered deeply from the harassment inflicted by her husband's family, which led to misunderstandings in the marriage. Eventually, the situation resulted in the fateful decision to sell her land in Skrobów and then move to the Colony when Lidia was about seven years old.

One day when Lidia wasn't even six, she felt tempted by the mysterious white birch grove she had glimpsed behind the hut where the two elderly people lived. She thought and thought about it, and then she set off on foot. That's where something strange happened to her.

Lidia couldn't follow the long route her father usually took, so she decided to find the grove on her own, vaguely remembering her older sister talking about approaching it from the opposite direction. She came to a clearing filled with sunshine. In the woods, only scattered rays flashed through the white birches, as if inviting her to play hide and seek. Shadows and light were jumping like bunnies, as when her older sister played at catching sunbeams in the mirror. Hadn't her sister said that there was a white grove behind the pear tree and the hut? And behind it a wide ditch filled with water, then a meadow with high grass where storks waded? It's probably even further, Lidia thought, looking around the green clearing.

Suddenly, she saw a small foal, white as the bark of the surrounding trees. It hopped as if playing hopscotch, but without paying attention to its legs to avoid landing on the wrong square. A white mare was nibbling next to it. Pretty as in that painting in the church, Lidia thought. Every now and then, the mare raised her beautiful head and neighed. Her call—Lidia liked the neighing of horses—was directed at the foal, which would then turn towards its mother and move closer. Lidia, a child herself, followed it with her hand outstretched. She thought she understood the mare's voice. Now the foal turned to her, looked with its big beautiful eyes, then bucked and set off at a gallop.

Without thinking, Lidia began to run, faster and faster. She and the foal ran side by side around the mare. The mare stopped nibbling at the grass; looked up, alarmed; neighed once and then again, each time louder. Girl and foal moved in ever-widening circles, as if propelled by the neighing. Lidia ran, spellbound. With her bright dress floating beside the white foal, they were almost one. The mare's whinny grew louder and louder. Suddenly, someone's hands grabbed and held Lidia both gently and firmly. Lifted up, she felt the earth still spinning. The hands carried Lidia to a place where a long, thatched roof almost touched the threshold of an entrance hall through which the hands carried her and seated her on a bench between a table and the window.

A melodious voice spoke from beneath a long, white beard. "The little miss needs an herbal infusion to strengthen her heart. She ran too fast and too long, racing with a foal. It is a prophecy for long journeys: she will—"

Lidia did not hear any more; she was half-asleep. She felt her hair being stroked and the soothing conversation of the two elderly people whom she considered her grandparents. Above all, however, she wanted to sleep.

Daddy appeared unexpectedly. She was drinking hot tea that smelled of mint and thyme while the old man described her adventure with horses. He finished, saying, "You have to guard her: you have chosen her to take a place of a son...."

Without listening further, Daddy took Lidia out of the room and put her on the straw-lined cart that was pulled by the chestnut mare that Lidia did not like. She was afraid of the mare's teeth and hooves. The elderly couple escorted her, saying goodbye with the sign of the cross. The cart rolled away, swaying and rumbling, more and more.... She fell asleep with the image of the concerned faces of the two people whom she loved. She would never see them again. Her father didn't take her there anymore, and she was not allowed to go by herself. A year later, she left the area with her parents and sisters.

Then came the war and the end of her childhood. In those terrible times, very hard for her family, she sometimes dreamed of the good, caring couple who were so dear to her and who had protected her. She was also curious about the meaning of the words spoken by the white-bearded man to her Daddy after the interruption of her dangerous run in the enchanted circle. A prophecy about distant travels?

Yes indeed. Lidia always liked travels by any vehicle, including plane and ship, their rocking and swaying. At times she considered what it meant that her father chose her, especially because he often demanded more from her than from her sisters, and he let her get away with more, even with all his severity and high expectations. She was his little girl, he trusted her; he knew that she would not let him or anyone else down, including herself.

A Girl on a Horse and Her Knight

The horse reared,
the girl pulled back the reins,
the animal pirouetted as if in a dance,
lowered its front legs to the ground,
and then they galloped away.

Scene I

Without looking her in the eye, one of the boys punished by her father said, "I'm proud to be punished."

Lidia was ashamed and sorry that she had complained. She did not know why she had done it. Actually, it was not certain that the boys had wanted to beat her up. They had ignored her sister, but they surrounded Lidia. The boys from Lipowa Street with whom she often played, as there were no other girls her age, used to surround whomever they wanted to beat up like that. Now these were the locals, on their home turf. She was new here and helping her sister bring the cows home from the pasture for only the second time. And this boy with a somber face was telling her that he was proud of being punished. Before running away, he added that he would have preferred to defend her—but didn't get the chance. She did not have the opportunity to ask what the words meant. A week later she was there again, but did not see him, and then she moved away with her family.

Scene II

An elderly man whom Lidia met in Konstancin, a small spa town known for its microclimate and treatments for patients recuperating from serious cardiological problems, shared a childhood memory with her. "Once, a long time ago, I saw something unforgettable. I was just over ten years old at the time. A young girl rode on a horse without a saddle, her bare legs and pigtails moving to the rhythm of the horse's movements. From the dirt road, they galloped

9

through the pasture in the midst of the frightened cows, straight towards a big tree. Right in front of the tree, the horse reared and then, pulled back by the girl with the reins, turned like a dancer, dropped his front legs, and raced back to the road. They quickly disappeared from sight. We stood, I and a few boys, bewitched. I do not know why we thought that the girl had simply wanted to show off.

She had such a remarkable face, full of light, and I could not turn my eyes away from her. This is what has remained with me forever, the enchantment.

The guys threatened that the next time they saw her, they would 'test' her to see if she was a witch. When, two days later, she came to help her sister with the cows, they rushed towards her. I ran with them, wanting to defend her, ready to fight the boys. I saw the same brightness on her face, suddenly tightened. She ran to the tree and began climbing it, like a squirrel. Then some passersby saw what was happening and drove the boys away."

Scene III

The first walk along the familiar river brought Lidia memories from the distant past. She realized that many events in her childhood had included horses. They were not always pleasant events, such as the gallop on the frightened horse that had carried her to the distant pasture. She could not recall whether it was Kasztanka, who bit and kicked dangerously, or another equally anxious mare. She remembered only that the animal set off at a racing pace, all the way trying to shake her off. Fortunately, it was a tame horse, and she held the reins in her hands. Her hands, however, were too weak to be fully effective in controlling the horse. At a gallop, turning at a sharp angle, they ran into a herd of grazing cows. Then, in front of them, Lidia glimpsed a huge tree.

The horse will hit the tree head-on and die, she had thought. Terrified, she pulled back on the reins until she saw the mare's head above her own face. She clung to the animal with her legs and arms. At some point she stopped feeling the sharp hair of its mane in her mouth. The leather reins stiffened, slicing into her palms; the horse turned in a semicircle and set off back to the house. In spite of her frightful experience, Lidia sensed that she was being watched by the boys guarding their cows. Afraid of being ridiculed, she tried not to reveal what was really happening to her.

Too bad that she did not find out back then that she had looked like a proud horse rider in full control over the galloping horse. And that one of the boys was so impressed with her that he was ready to defend her against the other, dangerous boys, to "fight for her."

Only now had she made the connection between that childhood incident and the story that the elderly gentleman she met in Konstancin had told her the previous year. She realized that she had been deprived of the feeling of elusive happiness, what being a girl means when she sees herself in the eyes of a boy.

Through Snowdrifts

Snow crunches with frost,
wind hurls sharp flakes
into the hair of horses' manes,
binds people's and horses' legs in snowdrifts.

On foot, it was possible to get to school through the fields or on a path trodden at the edge of a bushy incline. Scattered houses belonging to the village spread beyond the thicket where the slope descended into a flat area. The village of Zakrzów probably took its name from its location: "beyond the bushes." In 1936 a so-called "Colony" of three new farms appeared between the buildings of the village and the Manor estate on an area cut out of the estate and sold by its owner. The bare plot of land that was furthest from the estate and closest to the village was the new residence of Lidia's parents. This proximity to the village turned out to be a curse. The villagers believed that the fields should be theirs and considered the purchasers of the three plots to be intruders. They intimidated the Colony's inhabitants physically and psychologically, including through assaults and raids. The new arrivals, equally poor, were helpless and vulnerable. In the case of Lidia and her sisters, the harassment was particularly painful; the lack of brothers meant no defense. The fact that they were still children made things worse, for they could easily be frightened or even beaten up. Fortunately, at first the children did not understand everything, and as they grew up and understood more of the situation, their ability to cope improved.

Lidia matured amazingly fast. She learned to overcome her fear of local people, animals, and the elements. She did not have time or strength to remember the family seat in Skrobów; it seemed so far removed that it now felt unreal. She was still a child, and every morning except for Sundays she had to cover a distance of about four kilometers to school and then the same way back home, regardless of the weather: rain, frost, or blizzard. Lidia did not feel unhappy about it; she concentrated on her chores at home, making it to school, and learning all there was to learn. The school was dear to her, and she knew that it was her only way out to a different life, further education, and learning about the world. So, she went through the snow drifts, telling herself fairy tales she invented. In many of them, the heroine faced and conquered difficulties.

Often she was tired, weak, cold, and afraid when, on her way back through the field or on the path along the wall of bushes in autumn and winter she heard something rustle, crackle, hoot, wail. Most of all, she was afraid of people capable of harming her. Bad people appeared in fairy tales just like they did in real life all around her. In neither place did they protect children. To the local people, her family was foreign. Her sisters had been beaten up several times.

This time, she did not think about people. She trudged through deep snow, struggling to pull out her sinking legs. "Hindering" snow, it was called, a kind of thick, multi-layered snow that offered no footing. It was getting harder and harder to pull her legs out of the deep banks. Her fatigue grew. In the morning on her way to school, there was also a strong, frosty wind tossing snow and forming high snowdrifts. The drifts grew much bigger during the several hours she spent at school.

The snow kept falling, painfully striking the tensed skin of her face with sharp chunks. To protect herself from frostbite, Lidia tried to rub her face with snow that she warmed in her palms. She could not keep up with warming her hands inside her coat. Frost and wind reached everywhere, her red and blue hands hurt more and more, and it was getting harder and harder to breathe. She was resolved not to give in to weariness. She remembered stories about people who froze to death when they paused to rest. A few more steps, she thought, to the hill where there would be less snow, because there the wind would blow it away. She kept trying, but the thick snow would not let her take those few steps. Lidia searched for strength. Somewhere deep inside, she was convinced that she would not die, although she could no longer see clearly. Her mind began to drift. She couldn't tell whether an early twilight was descending or the snowstorm was dimming everything.

Suddenly, something showed in the distance. And it moved. Hope dawned when she thought that maybe someone was walking, maybe in the same direction as she was. Together it would be easier to proceed. Oh, the other person had stopped…. Lidia was not afraid, and she did not think she was delirious; after all, her fairy tales sometimes became reality.

In front of her, she saw an animal similar to a horse, not tall but thick, shaggy, the color of dirty snow. She remembered the images of various horses in books, and one of them was the spitting image of this one. Where did it come from, she wondered, hesitating; then she realized that the animal was leaving tracks. She reached them. The horse, yes, definitely a horse, she thought, was moving slowly forward, making holes in the deep snow. So, she followed, placing her feet in those footprint holes. The animal headed towards the shrubs, very tall in these parts. In front of them stretched the slope of the hill from which the wind always swept the snow away. Here, too, the layer of snow was much thinner. Lidia was glad to feel the ground under her feet again; now it would be easier.

A small, grizzled horse cut across the slope of the hill, and before she realized what had happened, it plunged into the thicket of bushes. She felt sad, as if she were losing something. Indeed, she could not see the horse anymore. She seemed warmer, maybe because she was moving, or maybe the wind had calmed before sunset. I hope not to get frostbite on my legs, she thought, feeling them freezing in her boots. She also worried about her hands and face, especially her face, because it would be blue and ugly. But above all, she was happy that she was already close to home. She was proud to have seen a wild horse. Yes, she convinced herself, it was definitely a wild horse.

The Summer of Signs in the Sky

A red glow filled the windows and flooded the interior of the house. Suddenly awakened, her parents jumped out of bed, fearing a fire. However, the building across the yard stayed dark, a large lump against the red background. The redness spilled around it. Seeing that, her parents figured that they were witnessing a supernatural phenomenon—signs in the sky that filled them with terror and the promise of something terrible. They awakened their eldest daughter so that she could remember the sight. And she remembered forever. Torn from sleep, seeing the expanding flames outside the window, at first she could not fathom why her parents did not try to extinguish the fire. It was only when she ran outdoors that her mother's words about signs in the sky heralding a war caught up with her.

A great white eagle appeared against the blood-red background. How clearly she could see the details: the feathers of its wings; its claws and beak; and its large, expressive eyes looking at her piercingly. Later the eagle turned into a huge, burning cross accompanied by columns of fire. The phenomenon lasted a long time and the onlookers, depending on the moment of their awakening, glimpsed different stages. Her parents remembered most the momentous, burning cross that engulfed the sky and the earth with flames. "There will be war," they proclaimed in unison.

WAR: the word, as unknown to her as the burning signs in the sky, scared the teenage girl. She was overcome with despair, similar to what she would feel a year later when her fiancé was killed in the first days of the war.

Staring at the silhouettes of her parents against the flaming background, she thought: it's good that my little sisters are asleep. Among them slept Lidia, ignorant of the signs that foretold the fate of her country, her family, and herself.

II

A Little Green Ball

tossed like a prize
at a toddler's feet

plays green on green
touches the fingers

leaves too soon
the longing hands

rolls on rolls on
a winding ribbon

sinks into darkness
revives in dawn

sparkles the braids
of a teenage girl

runs down in tears
of a woman's defeats

rolls on rolls on
in happiness glows

dims in grief
returns in wisdom

settles in the heart
free like the heart

keeps it from doubting
a little green ball

rolls on rolls on

The Girl and a Pheasant

In the little girl's hands
Beauty
On the gorgeous neck
Feathers
Gleaming with colors
The tail
Of long turquoise
Wilts
The terrified bird
Trembles
In the trapping hands
Their pulses
And his heartbeat
Unite—the throb
Of fear
Of bird's fate
The snare
Is open now, the moment
Eternity
And gift of freedom
Joy—
Girl's empty
Hands
And the free
Pheasant
Lift in the air

An Encounter with a Little Hare

A summer wind brushes Lidia's shoulders
warming her through the dark-blue school uniform
as she turns down a path
concealed among ripening grains, the last stretch
of her long walk back from school

Rye reigns here, high
thick stalks, good for making a fife
she stretches out her hand
a small fur-ball rolls out from the fields of grain
shivering it cuddles up to her legs

The girl crouches low, her pleated skirt
covers the little hare
the turmoil of a fiercely barking
pack of hunting dogs
rushes by, nearly knocks her down

Where did the hunters and their dogs come from?
she waits for the danger to recede
the bunny trembles at its savior's feet

Lidia still feels the hare's terrified heartbeat

Call of the Falling Night

The cord on the aluminum pail
quiets in the embrace of well's shaft
The glowing charcoals of dog's eyes
illuminate the path from the well
soothe the thickening darkness
that makes it harder to carry
water swaying in the bucket

The entrance door to the cottage shows up in grey

Darkness crawls with anxiety
toward *Wilczyca* tethered in her dog house
a link breaks in the strained chain
Suddenly free the she-wolf-dog lunges
catches the hand of the girl carrying water
and runs toward the forest

Pain and loss immobilize the girl
Her hand will not get to stroke her friend's rough fur

In the Horses' Dark Manes

snow sparkles
with flickering lights
of dancing stars
colliding with
freezing breath
of wind
horses
people

frost needles hurt
the wind
the horses
the people
they hit eyelids
settle
on eyebrows, lashes, hair
horses' manes

form
silver hoops
around nostrils
that try to catch air
before
it turns into crystals
of ice

with their hooves
horses strike pellets
coalescing in the goblets of snow

a girl fights
the urge to rest
the disabling faintness
that seizes
forces her to nestle
in the downy snow
that covers the hard earth

the struggle persists
till horses' nostrils sense
human breath

horseshoes flash
in the suspended movement of the hooves
snow scatters
from dark, mangled manes

Dark Lady

The night fades, hides the shadows, people rise
With dawn, look at clouds like angels' wings
Still laden with yesterday's toils and fears
They wait, unsure of new day's tales and trials

Rising sun's rays reveal powerful limbs
From horizon reaching out to heavens—
A giant, grown on marshland and legends
Dark Lady in a tree of old beliefs

Now I call that time wanting to reverse
From comforts to marshes on that bumpy
Path to glimpse the spring's reflection of my face

That spring water won't quench the thirst, only
Memory comes to my rescue, my true friend
When I long for morning, for its beauty

Jasmine

The fair night's blossom
the scent of rain
dogs' impassioned calls
my fear
under the spell
of storms of May

Oh, to happen again
upon that night
embedded in
jasmine scent

The Yellow Pitcher

The pitcher has been with me for decades
a yellow pitcher from my childhood on the hilltop
crept upon by vapors from the bog-meadows with sharp grass
blades hindering access to our little alders
which bore witness to my sisters' and my defenseless, heroic efforts
their moist leaves soothed bloodied legs

the alders in the meadows matured into big trees
often felled by the axes of robbers seen only by turtles
that hid in the swampy underbrush
amidst forget-me-nots and small mirrors of water

when howling winds and blizzards conquered our hill
and heaps of snow reached the leaden clouds that sprawled
to cloak the frozen windows, the sparkling pitcher on the cupboard shelf
brightened the dim kitchen

on hot days Grandma brought us a compote
made from red cherries or currants, like those
painted on the pitcher, and in the evenings
the music of crickets and croakers floated through the soft air

we lived our lives between the above and the below—
our animals sometimes tumbled down the slope, we pulled them back up to
    safety
we all depended on the buckets of water we had to carry up from the bottom
    of the hill

Leaving the hilltop house, I took with me the yellow pitcher
with its handle like a treble clef
and preserved inside, music that we all loved

And Now Only

longing
>	for a pheasant calling
>	frogs croaking
>	bees buzzing in white clover
>	dew drops on grass blades
>	sky-blue flax in bloom
>	wind enraptured with the scent
>	of ripening grains
>	and sun-warmed thyme

>	for the sight of the hill
>	now overgrown with the weeds of time
>	and human malice
>	branches of alders
>	marching from the river valley
>	like Birnam Wood
>	against fate

mourning
>	for the ruins of home
>	now protected only
>	by splinters of the ceiling
>	energy imprisoned
>	under a patina of mildew
>	in the wounded cupboard
>	standing sentry
>	at wall remnants
>	guardians of
>	memory

sorrow

      for lost lineage
      a table the hue of ripe cherries
      that guarded the family lore
      confided to paper
      secrets in black ink

      for the book of canticles
      opening with a song
      When the morning lights arise
      and closing with
      All our daily cares

Out of the Dream Dusk

Dusk falls in the stillness of forest
around the cluster of trees and brush
settles my thoughts

Feelings stream in from faraway times
reveal in retiring light
shadows of cows
in the meadows of remembrance

The closeness permeates:
fur odor after a hot day
chains rattling
a human connection

Strokes of the church clock
from a faraway tower
organize time

III

Memory Tapes

I stand on the tarmac at the airport in S.
There was a small country station out there
where the train tracks end

Suddenly on an airplane, all by myself
I fall into the seat by the window that opens
onto that landscape

I see a train on the tracks and what happened
long ago; I sense the wind touching petals
of tiny white daisies, and their scent

The girl on the steps of the train car
buries her face in a bouquet. Only the boy
offering the flowers is missing from the tape

And before that was wartime. I touch my travel bag

A tilt of the plane reveals dim woods, a country station
a ribbon of road, and a girl on an old bicycle. Above her
the fuselage of a metal bird with swastikas on its wings

and sharp eyes of the German pilot shooting at her
The thrust of the lowering plane pushes her bike off the road
hands of the knocked-down girl reach for the handlebar

The memory tape stops
I would like to bury my face in the bouquet of wild flowers
I want to free myself of childhood war memories

I Patted a Hedgehog

Gransee, 1980

At the outskirts of a German village
like a *Landschaft* embroidery
a hedgehog paused as if frozen in a frame
in his armor of upright spikes
which he gently laid down upon my touch

I patted a hedgehog at the outskirts of a dusk-wrapped
German village. In the background, green
fields sown with wheat, woods where tanks
stood at the ready—post-war props
with soldiers from the East, guarding

I patted a hedgehog, his spikes at rest
without awareness deeper
than the mood of a summer's evening
idyllic landscape and the silence in which
people can peacefully go to sleep

On Tree Branches

outside my window
in winter
crows grow
instead of leaves
stems/legs
cling to frozen branches
leaves/crows
go away   return
passing   transient

Dream or Not a Dream

A street
A sidewalk. Or perhaps the earth?
Something overpowers me
Immobilizes
Black clouds above

Dread!
Suddenly the skies open
A big, black horse falls down
In front of me

The earth trembles
Something bursts
The breathing...My breath returns
The nightmare slides off my chest
Calm

           Black horse...
           Danger...
           Back in my childhood
           A black mare, my *Karuńka*, jumping across the river
           Saved me

I wake up
I wake up to life

A New Day Is Rising

Rays of the freshly awakened sun
split the sickbay window panes
Outside, birds
open the world to a new day

Two seagulls hover above dwellings
stretched along the Baltic shore
in effortless, persistent flight
praising the morning lights

They soar in the realm between
the azure of the heavens and the earth
and the water with its music
unfinished over thousands of centuries

All day long, till the red-golden rites of the setting sun
the free creatures will act out their lives
Before sleep comes, the birds will circle once more
all the daily cares of the town till dusk's embrace

Before It Comes

Twilight crowing falls
on benches in the park

crows in their nests
hoarsely summon night's blackness

Waiting for the night
to take on the color of their feathers

they perform their parental tasks
loud love and care

drown out the music of the open beaks
of their young ones

The hubbub in the tree apartments fades
Calm descends

I, Homo Sapiens

the most important
inhabitant of planet Earth

sad, insecure, in a hurry
I curse the obstacles

envy the unreachable stars
with their billions of years

I look at the world from an upright position
climb trees, mountains, horses

given no wings by the creator
I invent the airplane

not as loyal as a horse
part of the team that pulls

I, a human
a woman, a man

in constant competition
a team overloaded

with excess obligations
under a banner that proclaims

life, battle, work, happiness
with their shadows and light

touched by love
I reach the stars

I See You

Kołobrzeg, 2005

where the sea rises up
and the flattened shadow like a bayonet
separates it from the horizon

a furrowed face shows
with eyes, the blue-gray of your eyes
transmitted to the sea
looking at me

on this side
the water casts wrinkled nets
of eternity—
millions of years
history of the universe
a moment
in one man's history

the waves swell
carry away your image
and the ground from under my feet

Freezing, Like Live Flowers

The snow is falling hard today—
ice chunks resist my legs
and blind me with stark whiteness

In those winters with you
the snow fell like magic
dancing down
glittering little stars
chased by my feet and eyes

And the red tulips
from street vendors' tables
stark stiff from the frost
in the warmth of the home softly melted
on the open lips of the vase

I am freezing, like live flowers
in the February chill

The Moon above the Wild Apple Tree

Suddenly I find you
peeking into the apartment's windows—
the moon
suspended above the wild apple tree

you reside on the moon
whose growing and fading
we used to follow
from our balcony

but this cold glare—
I search for the warmth of your eyes
when you stood beside me
in the dazzle of the full moon

today in its next phase
with a hazy ring predicting bad weather
the moon glances uncertainly
from the depth of secret shadows

you did not hide deeply
you had no liking for
rocky craters, waterless deserts
and you needed my presence

A Silhouette Showed on the Horizon

a lonely child
mothers worried

a lonely woman
men anticipated

a lonely man
women guessed

the figure kept growing

the pulsating horizon
followed as if in fear
for the human's fate

it's not a child anymore
the mothers relaxed

probably not so young
the men lost interest

needs help or poses a threat
the women pondered

the figure rested
on the quivering line

and became an unknown

The Memory Leaf

remains stubbornly on the branch
as though time were on hold

the window pane lets us see
does not ask why or wherefore

oh
to stop time
clasped to the branch

to save the memory
of the historian

wizard of medieval maps
poet with a camera lens

who each year
fall after fall

photographed the last leaf
to shield it against forgetting

Professor Tadeusz M. Nowak in memoriam

The Black Horse

turns his raised head towards the arriving people
tosses his unruly mane
can't rein in shivers galloping
under the tensed skin

hooves begin to dance
nostrils distend
catching the wind outside
the stable's window

the people, they are leaving
his throaty neigh resounds with
longing
desire
wrath
—gallops above trees of the old park
chasing the departing poets

The Forest Calmed

tinted by the sleepy sun
scattered yellow pine needles
on half-extinguished summer's green

my feet wade into soft stillness
marked only by somnolent
autumnal light
stretching among tree trunks

birds fall into silence
human voice softens

To Find a Blade of Grass

in the desert
and underneath the blade
a life-sustaining crumb
for today
for tomorrow

so little, that it can't
not exist—
my vision, my yearning
to grasp a morsel of manna
in a bird's beak

enough for a simple life
when a small gray bird
with wings of the dove
keeps guard

Translator's Note

I'm fascinated by Lidia Kosk, her biography, and her literary oeuvre. My adventure in rendering her poems into English dates back to 1997, when "From Nowhere to Nowhere," my first translation, appeared in the literary journal *Passager.*

After translating over 100 poems for Lidia's two bilingual books, *niedosyt/ reshapings* and *Słodka woda, słona woda/Sweet Water, Salt Water,* and for publication in numerous literary journals in the USA, I've embarked on the unique project of orchestrating their translation into a variety of languages. In *Szklana góra/Glass Mountain* I brought together twenty-one translators from around the world to render the title poem into their mother tongues, among them minority languages. I have already reflected on my journey as a translator and my fascination with the craft in my book *Face Half-Illuminated,* which creates a dialogue between Lidia's and my own poems, crossing history, generations, and geographical borders.

This book, *Meadows of Memory,* represents a step in a different direction. In 2018, inspired by Lidia's new and unpublished poems, I was tempted to try something different; I dipped into her short stories, crossing over from one genre into the next. Aware of the centrality of horses in her life, I searched for her poems that featured them, and then I followed their lead to other poems. It's not a linear story. The pieces don't fit perfectly together. While playing with them I was not solving one particular puzzle. In childhood, I played with a puzzle consisting of six wooden blocks that featured pictures. Each surface of the block displayed a part of one of six animals. Assembling them could result in six complete animals, say, a zebra, or a wolf, or mixtures of them. Later on, it became more challenging, as photos got damaged, parts lost. Yet they remain in my memory to this day.

After selecting five prose pieces for translation into English (section I), I've decided to complement them with 25 poems. First, ten poems in section II, to follow the prose that takes the reader back to the girl's childhood. Then, the 15 poems in section III start with reminiscences of World War II. The war is forecast in the last prose piece, "The Summer of Signs in the Sky," and signals the end of childhood.

The girl, horses, and fairy tale elements drew my attention first. From the previous books I've added the translations that I felt belonged in *Meadows of Memory*, thereby filling in the remaining blank spots. After discussing the book with Lidia and hearing her reminisce about hiding the bunny chased by hunters' dogs, I commissioned a poem for section II. Lidia wrote the poem, and I translated it. It fits in neatly right after "A Girl and the Pheasant," in which she releases a trapped bird, which could have become food for her starving family.

Fifteen of the poems in *Meadows of Memory* are making their English-language book debut here. So is the prose, except for "Lily," which has been published before in a different translation and form.

Acknowledgments

My heartfelt thanks go out to all those who read various parts of the manuscript; to the reviewers who drew on it to write such thoughtful pre-publication comments; and to my husband Andrzej and my son Piotr Kosicki, my companions in my second motherland. Piotr, born and raised in the USA, has helped me in a journey that crosses continents, languages and generations.

Grateful acknowledgment is made to the following publications in which these works first appeared, sometimes in a different form:

"Through Snowdrifts" in *Orca, A Literary Journal*
"The Summer of Signs in the Sky" in *Orca, A Literary Journal*
"In the Horses' Dark Manes" in *Subtropics*
"Jasmine" in *The Gunpowder Review*
"And Now Only" in *The Dirty Goat*
"Out of the Dream Dusk" in *Loch Raven Review Five*
"Memory Tapes" in *Under a Warm Green Linden*
"I Patted a Hedgehog" in *Under a Warm Green Linden*
"On Tree Branches" in *Beltway Poetry Quarterly*
"A New Day is Rising" in *ArLiJo, Gival Press*
"Before It Comes" in *Notre Dame Review*
"Freezing, Like Live Flowers" in *Petals in the Pan; Kind of a Hurricane Press*
"The Moon above the Wild Apple Tree" in *Blue Lyra Review*
"The Memory Leaf" in *Catalan Annals of Literature: L'Aiguadolç, Revista de Literatura*
"The Forest Calmed" in *ArLiJo, Gival Press*
"To Find a Blade of Grass" in *Notre Dame Review*

"The Girl and a Pheasant"; "Dark Lady"; and "A Silhouette Showed on the Horizon," made their first appearances, sometimes in different versions and under different titles, in Lidia Kosk's bilingual book *niedosyt/reshaping*. "In the Horses' Dark Manes"; "Jasmine"; "And Now Only"; "Out of the Dream Dusk";

and "I See You," in a slightly different form, and a variation of "Lily," appeared in *Słodka woda, Słona woda/Sweet Water, Salt Water.*

About the Authors

Lidia Kosk

Lidia Kosk, poet, writer, educator, lawyer, and photographer, is the author of twelve books of poetry and prose, and two anthologies. Her collaboration with her daughter, the poet and translator Danuta E. Kosk-Kosicka, resulted in two bilingual volumes: *Niedosyt/Reshapings* (Oficyna Dziennikarzy i Literatów POD WIATR, 2003) and *Słodka woda, słona woda/Sweet Water, Salt Water* (ASTRA, 2009). The latter book has been translated into Japanese by Hiroko Tsuji and Izumi Nakamura, and published in Japan in 2016. Lidia collaborated with her husband, Henryk P. Kosk, on the two-volume *Poland's Generals: A Popular Biographical Lexicon* (Ajaks, 1998, 2001).

Her most recent book is *Szklana góra/Glass Mountain* (Komograf, 2017), edited by Danuta E. Kosk-Kosicka. The book comprises renditions of her poem "Szklana góra" in twenty-two languages, ranging from Arabic to Italian to Occitan to Russian, as well as to a work of visual art for the cover. The translators, hailing from several countries on three continents, were thrilled by the poem. Lidia's poem brought them all together to celebrate the power of poetry and connectedness throughout the world. Their distinct voices, following the words of their translations, can be heard in the second, 2019, edition of the book enriched with QR codes.

Recently, music professor Sal Ferrantelli composed the score for "Szklana góra." The world premiere performance of the song by the soprano Laura Kafka-Price was in May 2019 at the Arts Club in Washington, DC.

As was typical of her generation, Lidia Kosk came of age during World War II and survived first the Nazi occupation of Poland, and then the Stalinist regime imposed on Poland by the Soviet Union. Her poetry bears witness to history and at the same time is an affirmation of life.

Lidia's poems and prose have been published in literary journals and anthologies in the USA, Poland, Russia and Japan; discussed and reviewed in English-, Polish- and Japanese-language publications; and featured on public radio in the

USA and Poland, and in multimedia video presentations. In 2012, for Mother's Day, the National Public Radio station WYPR's *The Signal* broadcast a program featuring her, speaking from her Warsaw apartment, and her daughter-translator in the studio in Baltimore. Composer Philip A. Olsen translated a series of her poems into choral compositions and the McDonogh School choir has performed them in several countries, including the USA, Peru, Portugal, and Spain. Olsen's "Polish Triptych" comprising his three choral compositions to Danuta's translations of Lidia's poems premiered in Baltimore in May 2017. Lidia resides in Warsaw, Poland, where she leads literary workshops and a Poets' Theater (ATP).

For more see: http://gm.kosk.xyz/ and http://danutakk.wordpress.com/about-lidia-kosk/

Danuta E. Kosk-Kosicka

Danuta E. Kosk-Kosicka is the translator for two bilingual books by Lidia Kosk, nominated for various translation prizes. Danuta has also edited two books, most recently *Szklana góra/Glass Mountain*, featuring Lidia Kosk's poem in twenty-two languages.

Over the years, in addition to Lidia Kosk, she went on to translate various Polish voices, including Ernest Bryll, author of numerous volumes of poetry, plays, and prose; Wisława Szymborska, the 1996 Nobel laureate; and recently Marcin Świetlicki, a contemporary poet and musician, as well as Grzegorz Białkowski, a poet and physicist. Since 1997, over seventy of her translations have appeared in the USA, in journals including *Notre Dame Review*, *The Fourth River*, *Subtropics*, and the *Tupelo Press*; in various anthologies; and on National Public Radio. Her translations have also gone in the other direction, from English to Polish, leading to the publication of her translations of three Maryland Poets Laureate—Lucille Clifton, Josephine Jacobsen, and Linda Pastan—in Poland in 2006.

She is a founding member of DC-ALT (the Washington, DC area branch of the US national association of translators), which she has represented in events at the Writers' Center in Bethesda, MD, and at the Columbia Festival of Arts. She has organized and led translators' panels at the CityLit Festival at

Enoch Pratt Library in Baltimore, in 2014; and at the *Confluence: Translations in the Capital Area* conferences at Montgomery College, in 2015 and 2017.

Life in two languages, bridging the cultural divide between Poland and the United States, has allowed her the unique opportunity to translate poetry and to inhabit the distinctive worlds and linguistic idioms of those countries. At *Loch Raven Review*, as the editor of the poetry translations section, she has focused on bilingual publications, one language per issue. Since 2011 she has presented poets, and their English translators, representing 19 languages, as diverse as Portuguese, Contemporary Mayan, Italian, Kurdish, Catalan, and most recently, Ukrainian and Arabic. Born and raised in Poland, she arrived in the USA in 1980, after receiving her PhD in biochemistry from the Polish Academy of Sciences. The imposition of martial law in her motherland on December 13, 1981, was the reason that she settled permanently in the USA. She resides in Catonsville, Maryland. She is the author of the prize-winning poetry collection *Oblige the Light* (CityLit Press, 2015) and *Face Half-Illuminated* (Apprentice House Press, 2015). For more information see http://danutakk.wordpress.com/

Apprentice
House Press
Loyola University Maryland

Apprentice House is the country's only campus-based, student-staffed book publishing company. Directed by professors and industry professionals, it is a nonprofit activity of the Communication Department at Loyola University Maryland.

Using state-of-the-art technology and an experiential learning model of education, Apprentice House publishes books in untraditional ways. This dual responsibility as publishers and educators creates an unprecedented collaborative environment among faculty and students, while teaching tomorrow's editors, designers, and marketers.

Outside of class, progress on book projects is carried forth by the AH Book Publishing Club, a co-curricular campus organization supported by Loyola University Maryland's Office of Student Activities.

Eclectic and provocative, Apprentice House titles intend to entertain as well as spark dialogue on a variety of topics. Financial contributions to sustain the press's work are welcomed. Contributions are tax deductible to the fullest extent allowed by the IRS.

To learn more about Apprentice House books or to obtain submission guidelines, please visit www.apprenticehouse.com.

Apprentice House
Communication Department
Loyola University Maryland
4501 N. Charles Street
Baltimore, MD 21210
Ph: 410-617-5265 • Fax: 410-617-2198
info@apprenticehouse.com • www.apprenticehouse.com

www.ingramcontent.com/pod-product-compliance
Lightning Source LLC
LaVergne TN
LVHW051429080426
835508LV00022B/3316